oil
vinegar
jelly doughnut
FISH
stockpot
rolling PIN
Onion
mussels
big SHOE
salt + pepper
milk
herb bundle
This book belongs to
LOVE
measuring spoons
butter
colander
mortar + pestle
cognac
black tulip
Bay leaves
BasiL
Thyme
HERBS
8lb.
8lb.
bottle opener
television
EEL
banana peeL
USA
letter
flag

People who love to eat are always the best people.

—Julia CHILD

BON appétit!

the delicious life of Julia CHILD

by jessie HARTLAND

schwartz & wade books
* new york *

Thanks to my great friend Isabelle Dervaux for help with French translations on the endpapers. More *merci beaucoups* to Etienne Perrot and Coline Drevo for further help. Thanks to my agent, Brenda Bowen, for finding the perfect home for the book. So clever! And to my wonderful editors, Anne and Lee. Just the right amount of poking and prodding. And lastly, thanks to my mom, Dottie Hill Hartland, for fabricating for Xmas 1965 the brilliant French café dollhouse (complete with tiny food and menus in French!), which got me started on France, cooking, and Julia Child.

—J.H.

Visit us on the Web! randomhouse.com/kids

Educators and librarians, for a variety of teaching tools, visit us at randomhouse.com/teachers

Library of Congress Cataloging-in-Publication Data
Hartland, Jessie.
Bon appetit! : the delicious life of Julia Child / Jessie Hartland.
—1st ed.
p. cm.
Summary: A picture book biography of Julia Child, the famous chef—Provided by publisher.
ISBN 978-0-375-86944-0 (trade)
ISBN 978-0-375-96944-7 (glb)
1. Child, Julia—Juvenile literature.
2. Women cooks—United States—Biography—Juvenile literature.
3. Graphic novels. I. Title.
TX649.C47H37 2012
641.5092—dc23
[B]
2011018658

The text in this book was lettered by hand.
The illustrations were rendered in gouache.
MANUFACTURED IN MALAYSIA

10 9 8 7 6 5 4 3 2 1

First Edition

Random House Children's Books supports the First Amendment and celebrates the right to read.

She bubbled over with effervescence, spoke as if she had marbles in her mouth, and gleefully hammed it up in front of the camera.

She wrote a classic French cookbook that still sells oodles of copies.

Mastering the Art of French Cooking

She joined a SPY mission during World War II...

Mastering II

galantine

Kunming
Ceylon
Marseille
Top Secret
Oslo
Paris
Germany
D.C.

She created and starred in a pioneering TV show loved by millions.

The French Chef

...and later moved to Paris and learned to cook.

How did a gangly girl from Pasadena do it? This is her story.

Julia McWilliams is born in Pasadena, California, in 1912.
CALIFORNIA
PASADENA
Los Angeles
orange tree
She is the oldest of three children.
Julia
John
Dort
ALL are TALL.
Pasadena is a town with orange groves, palm trees, and lovely weather year-round.
The prankster also builds tree houses, rides her bike everywhere, and throws mud pies at cars.
Julia plays dangerous games on roller skates. This one is called "hooking."
PASAD
BUS COMPANY
She is a true tomboy.

The McWilliams family is wealthy. They even have their own cook.
The cook serves mostly meat and potatoes.
Julia's mom only makes dinner on cook's night off and can prepare exactly three dishes:
biscuits
codfish balls
and
Welsh rabbit
What the heck is Welsh rabbit?
It's a mix of
beer
cheese
mustard
that is cooked together and served over toast.
Nothing to do with bunnies.
whew.
Julia loves to eat! She is certainly
NOT one of those tedious picky eaters. You know the type.

Julia's
unusual
HEIGHT
makes
dancing class
awkward-
for the 1920s, anyway.

But it comes in
handy for basketball.
She is team captain.

What is her favorite
after-school snack?
A jelly doughnut!

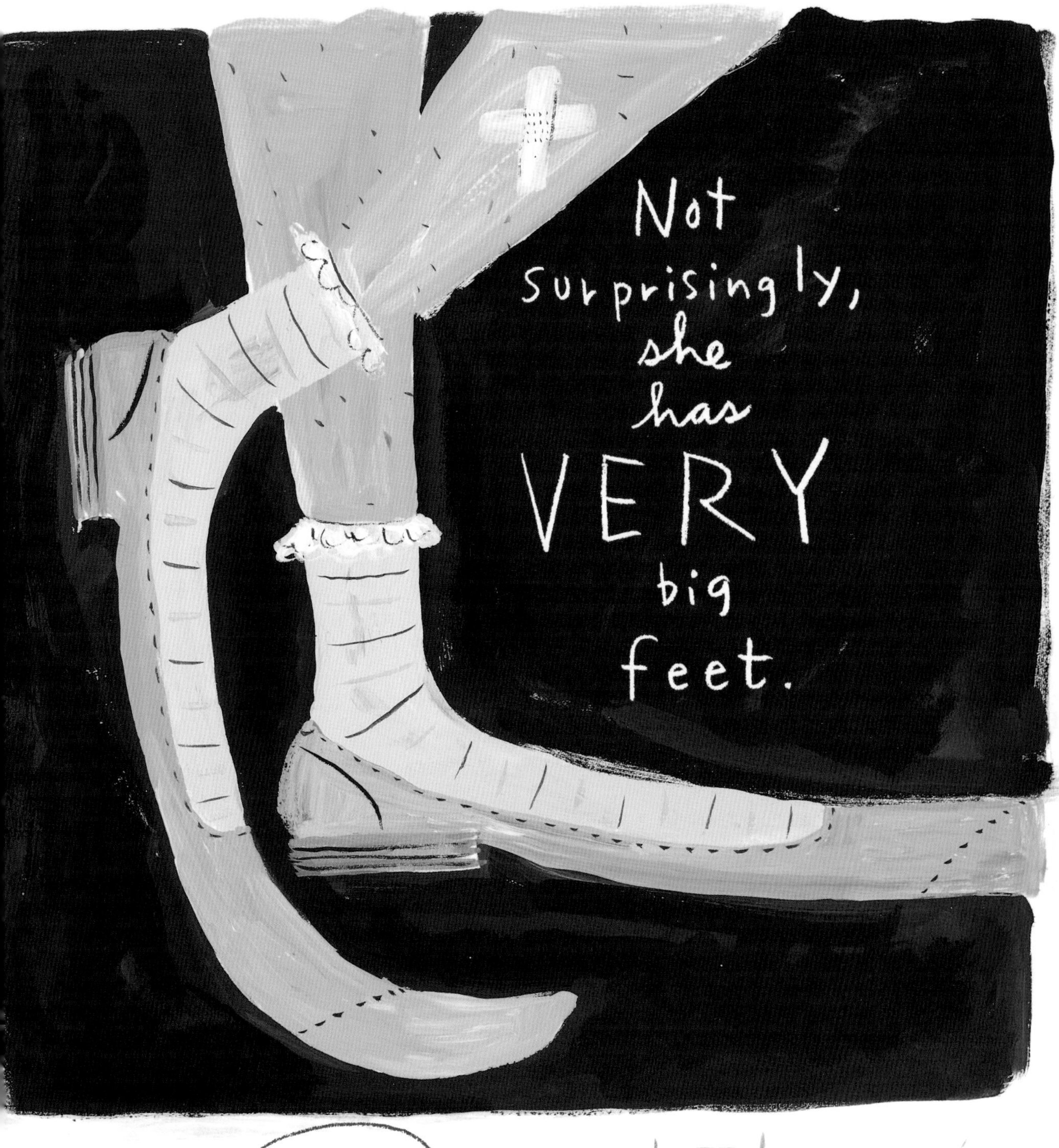
Not surprisingly, she has VERY big feet.

Do you have this in a size 12?
SAM'S SHOES

Julia is sent to the finest private schools and gets a great education, but she really doesn't take school all that seriously.

High school French class is a disaster.

(She will make up for this later.)

Just like her mom, she goes to Smith, an all-women's college in the East.

She is a hearty partier and still a prankster. She is famous for painting a toilet seat in her dormitory RED.

California U.S.A. Massachusetts

After college Julia moves to New York City to look for a job.

She flunks the typing test at

Newsweek magazine...

... but finds employment

at a large furniture store.

Her job is to write advertising copy.

Even though Julia likes to write, the job is kind of boring.

After a couple of years she moves back to California.

Her mom dies.

Julia takes a job at a new west Coast FASHION magazine.

But she is not interested in fashion.

Her traditional father expects that she will marry and settle into a conventional life in Pasadena.

But Julia wants something different.

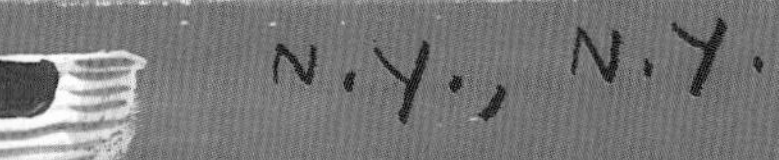

N.Y., N.Y. U.S.A. Pasadena

World War II begins. For the first time,

women are asked to join the armed forces.

Julia moves to Washington, D.C., and tries to enlist, but she is considered TOO TALL.

There is a new government agency, the Office of Strategic Services, and Julia gets a job with them.

She is shipped off to an island called Ceylon (now Sri Lanka).

The OSS is a spy agency. Julia likes to joke that

OSS stands for "Oh So Secret."

One of her projects is to help develop a shark repellant to keep curious sharks away from underwater explosives meant to destroy enemy ships.

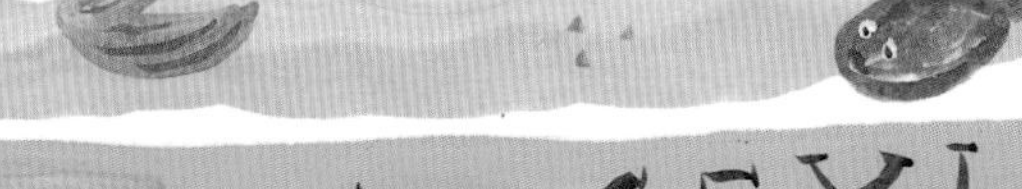

CEYLON

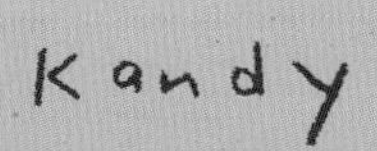

Julia's main job is organizing classified papers. She really likes her coworkers... especially
PAUL CHILD,
who is 10 years older and far more sophisticated than she is.
PAN
And what did YOU do before the OSS, Paul?
I was a teacher. I carved wood and made stained-glass windows. After that, I was a painter and photographer, and I lived in Paris.
Coincidentally, they both get transferred to China, where they like to try new restaurants together.
They have fish-head soup, ox tongue with tripe, snails, frogs, pig intestine, jellyfish with fish belly, pigs' ears with fish roe...
MENU
Let's order it all! I'm hungry!
When the war ends, they both move back to the United States.
They fall in love.
Kunming
CHINA
Kunming

Paul is a quiet, serious, cultured guy; Julia, a big friendly California gal. They complement each other.

Paul and his twin brother were raised by a single, artistic mom.

Julia and Paul marry in 1946. (Julia is 34.) (Paul is 44.)

Though it is unusual for the time, Paul supports the idea that a woman can have a career outside the home.

They move to a small house in Georgetown, a neighborhood in Washington, D.C.

In the evenings she tries to cook.

Julia works as a file clerk.

Paul works for a branch of the State Department, a federal agency. He plans and mounts exhibitions that aim to show the world what American art and culture look like.

Washington, D.C. U.S.A. Washington, D.C.

Julia and Paul are thrilled when the State Department offers Paul a job at the American embassy in Paris.
He will be running the exhibits office.
Un peu plus bas.*
*A little lower.
It is the perfect job for Paul—
he speaks the language already.
He loves everything French.
Paris is his favorite city in the world.
Julia has never been to Europe before.
PARIS
So they pack up all their things...
NYC
CEYLON
SMITH
CHINA
...in 14 suitcases...
and even take along the Blue Flash, their car...
S.S. AMERICA
for a weeklong boat trip across the Atlantic Ocean on stormy seas.

* Me too!

Le Havre FRANCE Le Havre 

La Couronne
Paul orders in FRENCH.
Qu'est-ce que vous recommandez ?*
* What do you recommend?
These are the best OYSTERS ever! The FISH is divine! The BREAD so crusty! The SALAD so crisp! The WINE is scrumptious! The BUTTER so rich! YUM! YUM!
Je prends ce qu'elle prend.**
** I'll have what she's having.
café-filtre
POUILLY-FUMÉ
sole meunière
huîtres
beurre d'Isigny
baguette
salade verte
fromage blanc
This meal is an AWAKENING for Julia.
Rouen FRANCE Rouen

Julia and Paul find an apartment at 81 rue de l'Université, on the Left Bank of the Seine River.
They call their place Roo de Loo.
In his spare time, Paul likes to draw and take photos.
This is Julia's cat, Minette.
81
Fête de la Musique
ART
JAZZ

Je m'appelle Frieda.
Their apartment comes with a femme de ménage, who cooks and cleans for them.
Paul and Julia don't like Frieda's cooking, so they let her go, and Julia begins to do a lot more cooking herself.
ooh la la!
Bonjour, monsieur.
Bonjour, madame.
Paris FRANCE Paris

kiosque

l'Arc de Triomphe

PAR

Armed with a map, Julia walks all over Paris, exploring sights and sounds and tasting new temptations.

Roo de Loo

le Louvre

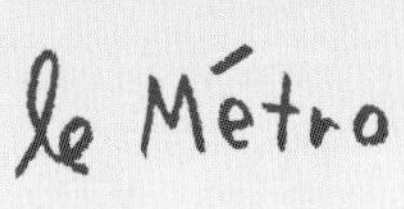
le Métro

l'Opéra

IS
la Tour Eiffel
MOULIN ROUGE
Julia spends the first months studying French. She loves to talk and believes that nothing is more important than being able to communicate. She works hard!
French
English
c
a
f
é
Berlitz
LEARN FRENCH!
Je m'appelle Julia.
Je suis américaine. J'aime la belle France!
Très bien!
BAR
TABAC
y'a bon
RIE
Fromagerie
CHARCUTERIE
It will take her two years to speak well enough to get by; four years to be fluent.
I love Paris!
dictionary
hard verbs
NOUNS
irregular verbs
impossible verbs
très difficile verbs
tre Dame
Sacré Coeur

Julia still wants a career and tries hatmaking. But it is not to be.
What does Julia really like to do?
EAT!
Someone suggests she take cooking classes. She likes the idea and enrolls at the famous Cordon Bleu cooking school.
LE CORDON BLEU
At first she is put into a beginners' class.
And now we all know how to make toast!
But after 2 days she transfers to a professional class.
Her classmates are 11 ex-WWII soldiers training to be restaurant chefs.

They learn how to make
Sauces
like béchamel
...Soups
like oignon
MILK
OIL
TEACHER
CHEF Bughard
...main courses
like
boeuf Bourguignon
BURGUNDY WINE
flour
...and desserts
like
crêpes Suzette.
BRANDY

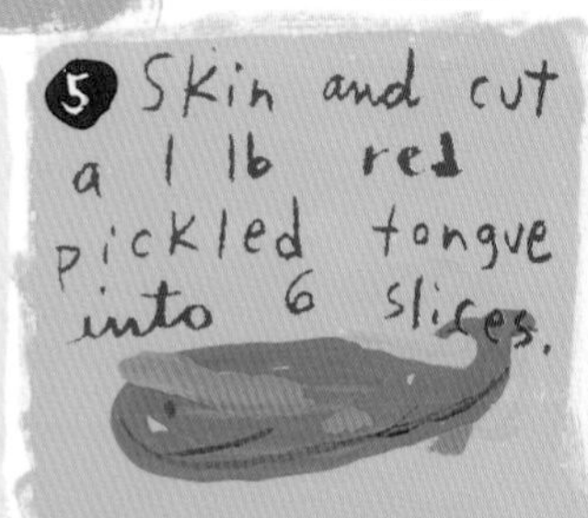

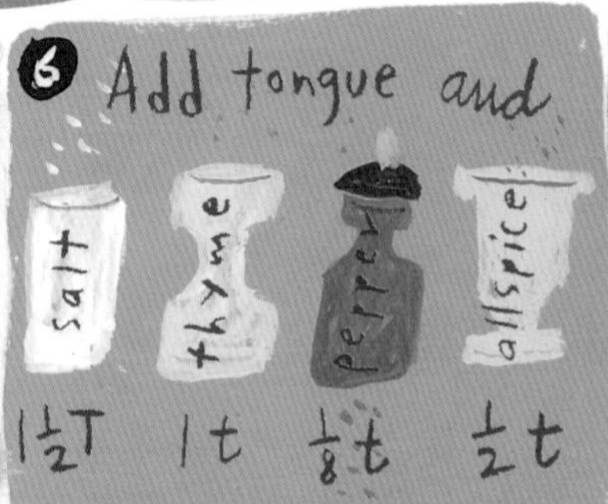

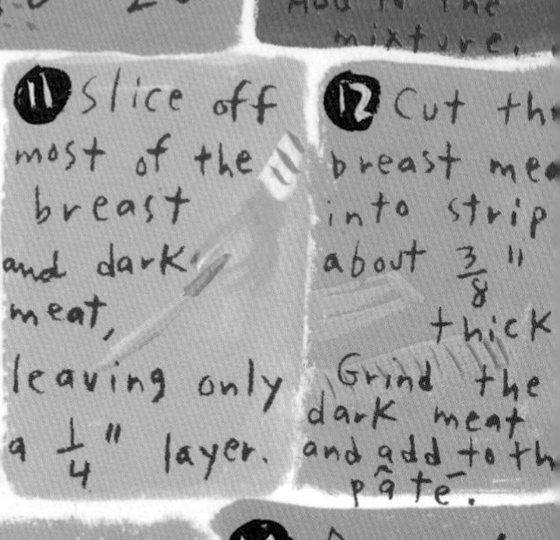

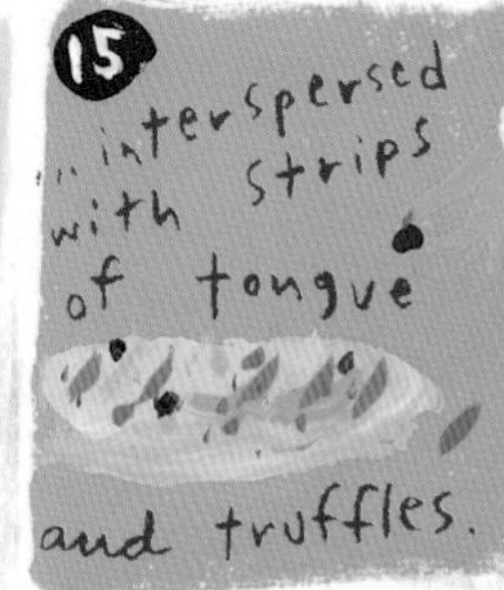

16 Repeat the layering until the pâté and the strips are used up.

** Truffles are fungi that grow underground.

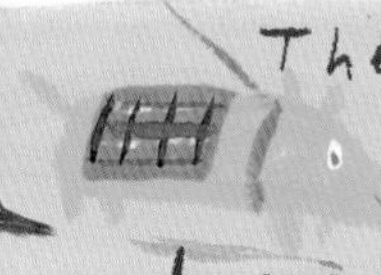

They are very precious and expensive because they cannot be cultivated and are found only in the wild.

17 Mold the chicken back to its original shape and
sew up with a trussing needle.
18 Wrap muslin around it
and tie the ends
with string.
19 Lay the chicken in a roaster.
20 Add 3 onions,
2 carrots,
and 3
celery stalks.
21 Season with a bay leaf,
2 t thyme, and 8 parsley sprigs.
thyme
22 Add the chicken carcass bones and, if you wish, some
veal knuckles and calves' feet.
23 Fill pan to 1 1/2" with chicken broth. Add a glass of white wine
and 2 T of old brandy.
old brandy
24 Cover the whole thing with a piece of buttered parchment paper.
Cook over a high flame and bring to a simmer.
25 Turn down the heat and simmer slowly for 3 hours.
Remove from the heat.
26 After an hour, lift the galantine out of the pan and
place it on a platter.
27 Cover with a lid and an 8-lb weight.
28 When the galantine has cooled, remove the string.
29 Remove the muslin, gently press out any juices, and dry the outside with a cloth.
30 Strain the jelly that has accumulated on the platter through a sieve, remove the fat, clarify it, and then brush it on. This is called aspic.
31 Put the galantine on a serving plate and decorate it with pimiento, blanched pistachios, pickled udder, blanched leeks,
truffles, and pickled tongue.
32 Finally, glaze with 2 more
coats of aspic.
Pigs and dogs are trained to sniff them out.
A black truffle this size can cost about $40.
actual size

Here's a little something I just whipped up!
Voilà!!!
La pièce de résistance!!!

Julia goes to lots of parties,
METRO
and at one she meets a French-woman named Simone Beck, nicknamed Simca.
SIMCA
Larousse Gastronomique
She also loves to cook, read about food, and talk about food.
Simca and her friend Louisette Bertholle
are trying to write a FRENCH cookbook for Americans, without much success.
Another rejection! Tant pis! *
Zut alors! **
* Too bad! ** Darn it!
One day Julia reads a magazine article by an American complaining about the lack of good kitchen knives in the United States.
HARPER'S magazine
In appreciation, she sends the writer two
Air mail
DeVoto
Cambridge, Mass.
U.S.A.
small French steel knives.
This is a pivotal moment.
A correspondence is started with the writer's wife,
AVIS DeVOTO.
A new pen pal!
is
Julia
AVIS
Julia!
avis
Julia
AVIS
Julia
vis
Julia
AVIS

In 1951 Julia graduates from the Cordon Bleu.

Julia and her friends Simca and Louisette start a cooking school of their own.

It's called Ecole Des 3 Gourmandes *

Paul designs the logo.

The classes are given in Julia's kitchen.

The students are mostly American women found through the embassy.

---

* "The school of the 3 Hearty Eaters."

Simca and Louisette tell Julia about their cookbook project.

Our publisher just rejected our book . . .

. . . but they asked us to rework it with an American.

Julia, will you help us?

Quelle bonne idée! * I'd love to!

* What a great idea!

She looks at the recipes they have already written.

These techniques should be explained more clearly! And crème fraîche and fresh tarragon? Americans can't find such things in their supermarkets! Why not redo this so that the recipes are FOOLPROOF and work with American ingredients and equipment?

Ah, oui.

D'accord.**

** Okay.

With Avis DeVoto's help, they make a deal with a new publisher in Boston, then set to work completely rewriting. They work hard.

After 4 years in PARIS, Paul's work takes him and Julia to MARSEILLE, a bustling port city on the Mediterranean Sea.
Belgium
Germany
PARIS
FRANCE
Atlantic OCEAN
Italy
MARSEILLE
MEDITERRANEAN Sea
Julia is sad to leave Paris but glad to still be in France.
BOX 2
BOX 7
They find an apartment with a view of the harbor.
Work continues on what Julia calls the "cookery-bookery."
I'm sending you the EGG chapter.
Julia Marseille
Simca Paris
I'm sending you the SAUCE chapter.
Paul and Julia tool aroun the South of France in thei new car, la Tulipe Noire*
Provence is my favorite part of France.
Moi aussi!**
PARIS
FRANCE
Provence
*The Black Tulip. ** Me too!
marseille FRANCE marseille

The fish market is right at Julia's door. She loves the famous mediterranean fish stew called bouillabaisse and wants to know how to make it.
BONJOUR!! I'm looking for the TRUE, classic bouillabaisse** recipe.
NO lobster!
NO Saffron!
It MUST have butter.
It MUST have mussels!
praires
huîtres
clovisses
moules
Never put in eels.
Pas de moules! *
Always—lobster!
Bouillabaisse MUST have saffron!
POISSONS
homards
MARSEILLE
* NO mussels!
** say "boo-ya-BESS"

Paul next gets transferred to Plittersdorf, Germany.
It's hard to pick up and move every few years so correspondence with friends is even more important!
Ich habe Hunger!*
PARIS
Julia sends Avis some shallots.
TIN FOIL
white FLOUR
CLAMS
Julia Child Plittersdorf GERMANY
AIR MAIL
Avis DeVoto USA!
Avis sends Julia authentic American ingredients (important for working out the recipes).
Julia and Simca exchange 60 pages of letters about whether preserved goose is essential to a French stew called a cassoulet
NON
NO Preserved GOOSE!
mais oui! goose
(Louisette has become less involved in the cookbook.)
GERMANY
EAST
West
*I'm hungry!
Plittersdorf GERMANY plittersdorf

The cookbook manuscript is HUGE and is still not complete. Their idea is to publish a new volume every year.

FRENCH RECIPES FOR AMERICAN COOKS

Washington, D.C. U.S.A. Washington, D.C.

Julia and Simca get a letter from Boston.
Rejected!
They want a shorter, simpler book. More shortcuts. Like using mixes and canned things...
HM
mon Dieu. Quelle horreur!* That's not French!
* my God. How appalling
I don't like the shortcut idea either. But we can still do a simpler book. Can't we?
Yes. Let's get to work.
bye!
au revoir!
Paul is next transferred to Oslo, Norway, for 2 years.
Julia works on her skiing, gives some cooking lessons,
and learns some essential Norwegian:
Jeg er sulten!*
*I'm hungry
NORWAY
SWEDEN
Oslo
EUROPE
Oslo NORWAY Oslo

Julia is working on the
FISH
RECIPES.
First she might try 10 existing recipes for one dish.
Hmmm... I think I can improve on that.
Poissons
Seafood
FISH
Voilà! A new (and improved) recipe!
Then she might rework it... and make it 8 times!
Tweak it.
Mmmm... mussels!
Cook it again.
Then she might develop a new technique.
And troubleshoot. How might cooks make mistakes?
Hmmm.... mussels.
more detailed instructions.
Mussels again?
Paul is the guinea pig.
Fine-tune it. Cook it 6 more times.
Julia is a perfectionist.
The final result? An original recipe! And it's foolproof.
Moules 7

That same year, when Paul retires from the State Department, he and Julia move to Cambridge, just outside Boston.

Paul grew up in Boston, and they already have friends in the area. They buy a house with a nice big kitchen.

Julia and Simca work hard to promote the new book—

They give demonstrations in department stores.

And they sign copies in bookstores.

They are interviewed on the radio . . .

*It's true, 10 yea

Cambridge, Mass. U.S.A. Cambridge, Mass.

. . . and on a rather new medium called TELEVISION.
They do a DEMO on a PBS book show.
WGBH
I've Been Reading
(At first, all TVs were just in black-and-white.)

So many people love the demo that Boston public TV station WGBH offers Julia her own cooking show.

Even people who don't like to cook watch the show and love it!

The TV show does not pay particularly well, but it is good publicity for the cookbooks.

And Julia's advice should something fall on the floor?

The shows are not live, but—to save money—they are all shot in "one take" (no editing), which is tricky.

There are some very funny moments.
1
Once Julia pulls a used bundle of herbs from a stockpot and says,
It looks like a dead mouse!
2
Another time she simply TOSSES an inferior loaf of bread over her shoulder.
No good! That bread!
3
Julia keeps all her favorite knives, scoops, and other tools in a special bag.
"The Sacred Bag"
4
Always Taste, taste, taste...
5
On the suckling pig show she carefully cleans the pig's ears and teeth before cooking.
PIG TEETH
toothpaste
6
But when it comes out of the oven she can't cut it into chops.
You try to carve it—I certainly can't!
7

WGBH
you have spinach in your teeth!
there's a pot holder on fire!
now crack 2 eggs
SMILE
These are called
stop gasping!
IDIOT CARDS
wipe your face!
now melt the butter
stop galloping!

Oh, nuts! I burned the sauce.
I'm Julia Child. Bon appétit!*
Don't apologize for your cooking mistakes. It is what it is.
Ecole Des 3 Gourmandes
*She ends each show saying this.

Julia Child is now famous! Her hard work has brought her great success, and this allows her and Paul to build a house in Provence, in the South of France.

She goes on to write many more books.

Because she is so tall, she has the kitchen counters custom-built so that they are higher.

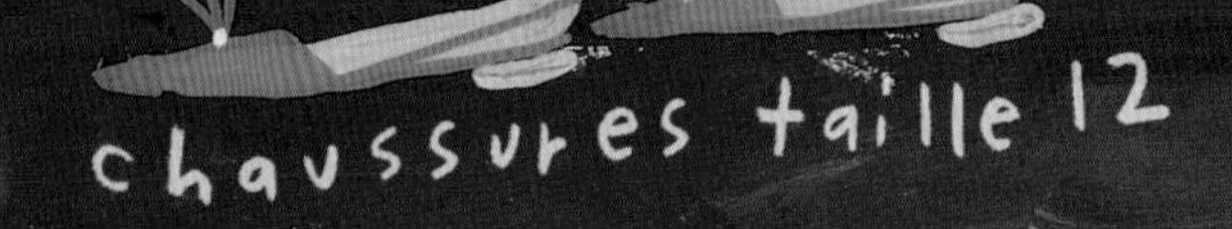

livre de cuisine
oie
galantine
requin
saucisson
chapeau
couteau-scie
Ecole Des 3 Gourmandes
truffes
fromage BRIE
noix
ail
oeuf
VIN
ciseaux
citron
chat
fouet
pomme
couteau
une pincée
manique
casserole
parapluie
cuiller en bois
sucre
homard
couteau
cochon de lait
Germany
CHILD
OSLO
PARIS
marsaille
valise
spatule
farine
tour Eiffel